CANADA WILD
ANIMALS FOUND NOWHERE ELSE ON EARTH

WORDS BY MARIA BIRMINGHAM
ART BY ALEX MACASKILL

NIMBUS
PUBLISHING LTD.
NIMBUS.CA

Nimbus Publishing Limited
3660 Strawberry Hill St, Halifax, NS, B3K 5A9
(902) 455-4286 nimbus.ca

The Nature Conservancy of Canada and NatureServe Canada report called *Ours to Save* lists the 308 endemic Canadian species and inspired this book. You can read the whole report and find out more at natureconservancy.ca/ourstosave.

NB1594
Printed and bound in Canada
Editor: Penelope Jackson
Editor for the press: Whitney Moran
Design: Heather Bryan
Cover design: Alex MacAskill

Library and Archives Canada Cataloguing in Publication

Title: Canada wild : animals found nowhere else on Earth / words by Maria
    Birmingham ; art by Alex MacAskill.
Names: Birmingham, Maria, author. | MacAskill, Alex, illustrator.
Identifiers: Canadiana (print) 20220239142 | Canadiana (ebook) 20220239150 |
    ISBN 9781774711132 (softcover) | ISBN 9781774711330 (EPUB)
Subjects: LCSH: Endemic animals—Canada—Juvenile literature. | LCSH: Rare
    animals—Canada—Juvenile literature. | LCSH: Endangered species—Canada—
    Juvenile literature.
Classification: LCC QL219 .B57 2022 | DDC j591.971—dc23

Nimbus Publishing acknowledges the financial support for its publishing activities from the Government of Canada, the Canada Council for the Arts, and from the Province of Nova Scotia. We are pleased to work in partnership with the Province of Nova Scotia to develop and promote our creative industries for the benefit of all Nova Scotians.

INTRODUCTION

Look No Further

With its vast landscape, it's not surprising that Canada is home to countless animals. Even so, when you hear the numbers, it's hard to imagine. From coast to coast to coast, you'll find about 50,000 species roaming the country! Just stop and think about that for a moment—all those species call Canada home.

Some of these animals are also found in other places around the planet. But there are those that only live here, in the "true North strong and free." All in all, there are 308 species—both plants and animals—that are uniquely Canadian. They're known as *endemic species*, meaning they don't live anywhere else on Earth.

Most of these animals live in a particular region within Canada. And many of them are threatened or endangered. That means it's up to Canadians to make sure these creatures survive and thrive in the future.

From birds to mammals to bugs to fish, let's meet a few of these uniquely Canadian species and see what's being done to keep them safe.

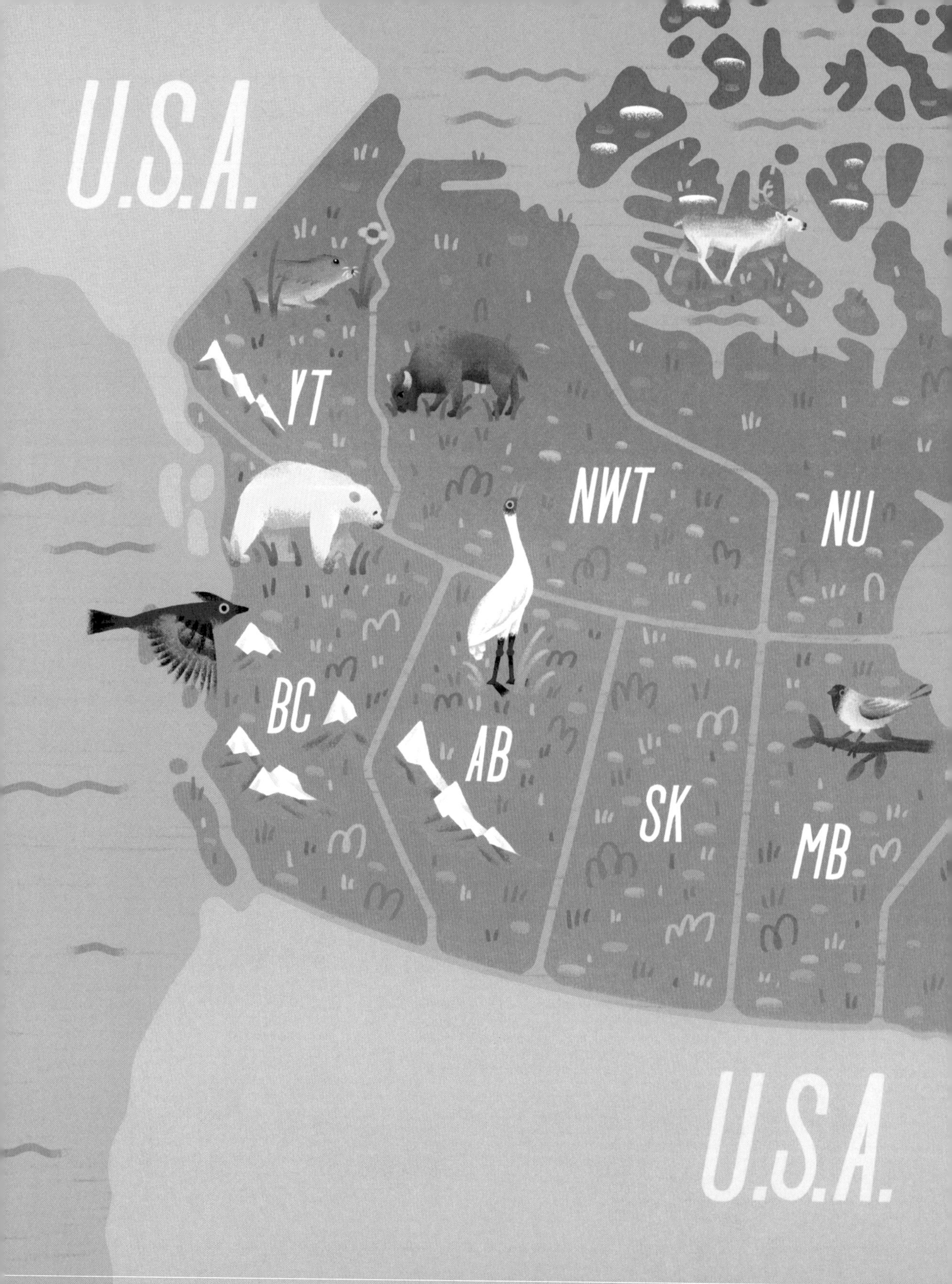
U.S.A.
YT
NWT
NU
BC
AB
SK
MB
U.S.A.

CANADA

NL

QC

ON

PE

NB

NS

WHOOPING CRANE

Habitat:	Wetlands of Alberta and the Northwest Territories
Diet:	Snails, aquatic bugs, minnows, frogs, and some grains
Status:	Endangered

It's hard to miss the whooping crane, thanks to its long neck, thin legs, and white body. Not to mention the fact that at 1.5 metres, it's the tallest bird in North America—about the same height as a twelve-year-old kid! There's only one flock of whooping cranes that lives and breeds in the wild without getting any help from humans. Made up of about five hundred birds, this flock is found in Wood Buffalo National Park, a spot along the border of Alberta and the Northwest Territories. While there are three other small flocks in the United States, they're part of breeding projects, so these whooping cranes aren't considered a natural population like the ones found in Canada. The wild Canadian flock, however, does travel to the US. The birds leave their nesting site each fall, migrating south to the coastline of Texas. They spend the winter and early spring there until it's time to make the long journey home to have their young in Canada.

FACT FILE:

◊ What's in a name? The whooping crane gets its name from its loud call, which can be heard from several kilometres away. It's also nicknamed the "whooper."

◊ The bird uses its wings to drift through the sky over long distances, like a glider. In fact, it can soar for up to ten hours straight!

◊ Whooping cranes usually build their nests in shallow ponds or marshes. That way, their chicks—which don't fly until they're about three months old—can quickly escape predators by swimming off.

◊ Just call the whooping crane the comeback kid. During the 1940s, there were only about twenty of these birds on the planet. Both Canadian and American wildlife teams began breeding the birds in rescue centres to save them from extinction. While the whooping crane is still considered endangered, these efforts have brought the birds back from the brink. There are now about six hundred of them living in the wild and captivity.

HOW'S IT DOING?

Whooping cranes face several dangers to their survival. They can be harmed when they collide with power lines during their migration or when flying into severe weather. And sometimes they are mistakenly hunted by humans. One of the biggest threats to the birds is the loss of their habitat due to development. But a lot of people are working to help the whooping crane: it's now a protected species in Canada and the US, and its breeding grounds in Wood Buffalo National Park are protected too. Wildlife groups are also working to protect the whooping cranes' habitat along their migration route, which ensures the birds have stopover sites where they can rest and feed on their lengthy journey. And their wintering grounds in Texas have been a wildlife refuge since 1937 to ensure they remain safe through the season.

EASTERN WOLF

Habitat: Forests of central Ontario and western Quebec

Diet: White-tailed deer, moose, and rodents

Status: Threatened

The eastern wolf, also known as the Algonquin wolf, makes its home in forested areas, where it usually spends the daytime hours resting and sleeping. As night arrives, the wolf begins to search for dinner. It lives in a pack that includes several adults and pups. Most packs have up to ten wolves. The pack prowls its territory throughout the night, constantly on the move as it searches for its next meal. The wolves work together as a group to hunt their larger prey, following a target until the time is right to chase it down, surround it, and attack.

FACT FILE:

◊ The largest population of eastern wolves lives in Algonquin Provincial Park, which is found in southeastern Ontario.

◊ One of the ways a wolf communicates with its pack is by its low, long howl. This howl can be heard up to sixteen kilometres away and helps wolves tell other pack members where they are if the group becomes separated. It's also used to warn wolf packs to steer clear of other packs' territories.

◊ A program at Algonquin Park invites people to come to the park to learn more about the wolves and even hear them howl at a nighttime event. Sometimes these folks imitate a wolf howl and the wild wolves answer back!

◊ When pups are born, their mom nurses them in a den—like a small cave— for about two months. After this, the young are moved to an open area called a *rendezvous site*. Other pack members gather here during the day and night to help care for and feed the pups. By the time a pup is about six months old, it's ready to join the rest of the pack to hunt.

HOW'S IT DOING?

This species is threatened, which means that while it is not endangered, it's likely to become endangered in the future if things don't change. When it comes to the eastern wolf, its numbers have dropped over the past few decades. It used to be found in most of southern Ontario and the northeastern United States. But as we began to farm this area, hunting and trapping of the wolves reduced the population. Human activity, like building roads, has caused habitat loss and has also impacted the wolves' numbers. With fewer than five hundred eastern wolves left, the Canadian government has banned hunting and trapping of wolves in provincial parks and surrounding areas where they live and roam.

Habitat: Coastal rainforests of northwestern British Columbia

Diet: Berries, grasses, young deer or moose, and salmon

Status: Stable (Rare)

It may look a bit like a polar bear, but don't be fooled. This Kermode bear is actually a type of black bear. Even more confused? Let's straighten things out. While most Kermode bears are black, a rare few have white fur. That's because of their genes—the part of our cells that control how our bodies grow and work. Just like you inherit a certain eye colour from your parents, some Kermode bears inherit their unusual fur colour. These bears are often called a *spirit bear* or *ghost bear*. Whether it has white fur or not, the Kermode bear is a solitary creature. The exception is a mother raising her cubs. They travel together until the young are around two years old. Kermode bears spend their days roaming through the rainforest. When the winter months roll around, the bears hibernate for several months, often snoozing away in large hollow trees.

FACT FILE:

◊   Coastal Indigenous Peoples have known about the Kermode bear for thousands of years. In fact, they consider the bear to be a sacred creature. The spirit bear is known as *moksgm'ol*, or "white bear," in Tsimshian languages. And it is a part of several stories that have been shared for generations.

◊   The rest of the world learned about the existence of the Kermode bear in 1905 when an American scientist observed it during an expedition. He named it after a museum worker, Francis Kermode, who helped track down the species.

◊   The Kermode bear was named the official mammal of British Columbia in 2006.

◊ This mammal catches salmon from coastal waters and carries the fish into the forest, eating until it's full. The bear leaves its leftovers behind. These salmon remains feed some of the smaller animals that live in the rainforest, including mink, eagles, and even snails. And the leftover salmon also fertilizes the trees and plants. So you could say the bear helps its rainforest home grow!

HOW'S IT DOING?

It's believed there are fewer than five hundred white-furred Kermode bears in the wilderness of British Columbia. An agreement was made in 2006 to protect the Kermode habitat by preventing logging and hunting. Even so, the bear does face other threats. For instance, climate change, ocean pollution, and overfishing are causing the salmon population to drop. Salmon are an important part of the Kermode bear's diet. To make matters worse, they're also a favourite of other bears, like grizzlies. Now these bears are coming into the spirit bear's territory looking for more food. And that's leading to competition for salmon, which could mean less food for the Kermode bear.

UNGAVA SEAL

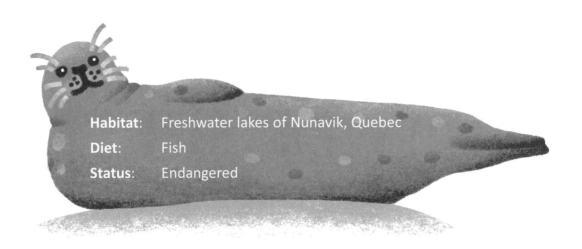

Habitat: Freshwater lakes of Nunavik, Quebec
Diet: Fish
Status: Endangered

Also known as the Lacs des Loups Marins harbour seal (now, that's a mouthful!), this creature lives in a series of connected lakes. Like other harbour seals, it spends part of its time in shallow water and part of its time on land. It can dive deep for prey and is able to hold its breath for up to thirty minutes at a time! And while it doesn't have ear flaps, it does have ear holes. They close up when the seal heads underwater. This swimmer often leaves the water, or hauls out, to settle on beaches or rocky shorelines. Here it rests, hangs out with other seals, and raises its young.

FACT FILE:

◊   The Ungava seal has short, webbed flippers with five claws, which are used for grooming and to scratch those hard-to-reach places.

◊   Its back flippers help the seal swim powerfully through the water. And its front flippers are used to steer its body.

◊   While it's a strong swimmer, the harbour seal can't walk well on land. It has to scoot along on its belly to move about, sort of like a caterpillar.

◊   Shortly after a seal pup is born, it's ready to swim. It makes its way to the water and takes a plunge for a few minutes at a time. If the pup gets tired, it may hop aboard its mom's back for a ride. Whee!

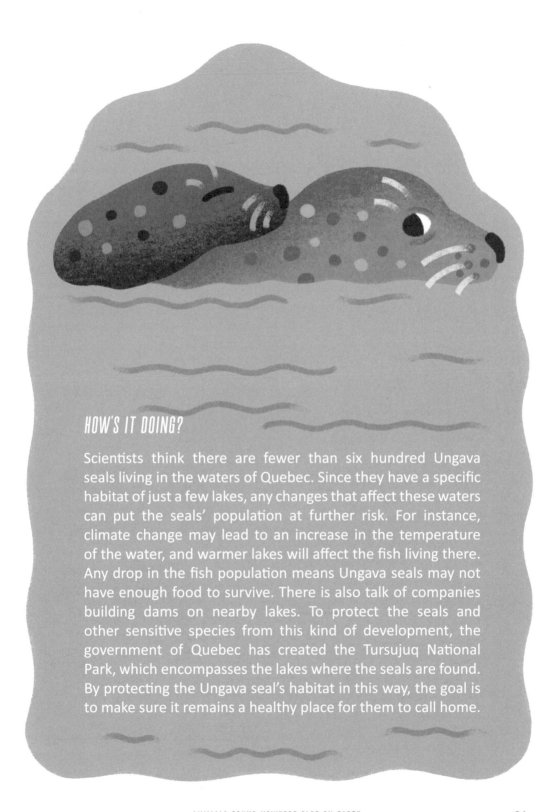

HOW'S IT DOING?

Scientists think there are fewer than six hundred Ungava seals living in the waters of Quebec. Since they have a specific habitat of just a few lakes, any changes that affect these waters can put the seals' population at further risk. For instance, climate change may lead to an increase in the temperature of the water, and warmer lakes will affect the fish living there. Any drop in the fish population means Ungava seals may not have enough food to survive. There is also talk of companies building dams on nearby lakes. To protect the seals and other sensitive species from this kind of development, the government of Quebec has created the Tursujuq National Park, which encompasses the lakes where the seals are found. By protecting the Ungava seal's habitat in this way, the goal is to make sure it remains a healthy place for them to call home.

SABLE ISLAND
SWEAT BEE

Habitat: Grasslands of Sable Island, Nova Scotia

Diet: Pollen and nectar from flowers

Status: Threatened

You'd think a bee could live anywhere it wants. After all…has wings, can fly! But the Sable Island sweat bee lives in just one spot: a small island three hundred kilometres off the coast of Nova Scotia. It can't fly far enough to reach land, so here it stays on Sable Island, along with wild horses, a few birds, and a handful of other bugs. That doesn't mean the sweat bee is easy to spot if you go looking for it, though. This bee is only about the size of an ant!

FACT FILE:

◊   Where does this bee get its name? It doesn't actually sweat. But some bees in this species like to drink the sweat they find on human skin. Thus, the name!

◊   Females of this species are a pale golden colour, with flecks of blue or green. The males are reddish brown.

◊   For a little bug, the sweat bee has a big job on its island home. It pollinates the flowering plants found here, including the blue flag iris, seaside goldenrod, and red clover. That means the bee takes pollen—the tiny grains in a flower that help produce seeds—from one plant and transfers it to another. This helps the plants continue to grow and thrive.

◊   According to experts, if sweat bees didn't pollinate plants on Sable Island, some plant species might disappear.

◊   This bee nests underground. A female digs burrows in the sandy ground where it lays its eggs.

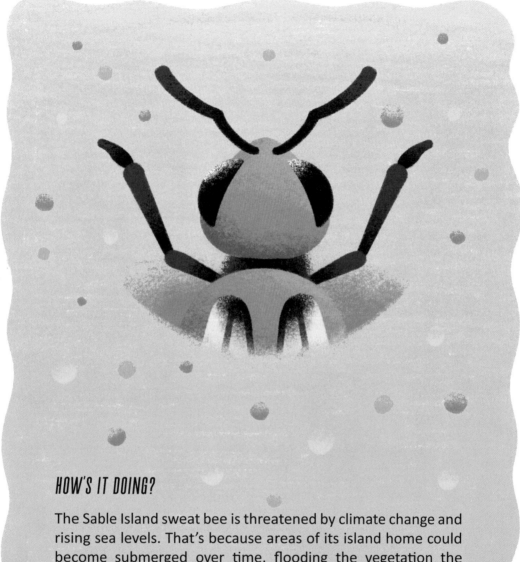

HOW'S IT DOING?

The Sable Island sweat bee is threatened by climate change and rising sea levels. That's because areas of its island home could become submerged over time, flooding the vegetation the bee needs to survive. As well, powerful storms have become more common in recent years, and these can also change the bee's habitat and disturb its population. Several researchers are working on the island to try and understand more about the species to see if they can come up with ways to protect it.

NEWFOUNDLAND
PINE MARTEN

Habitat:	Forests of Newfoundland
Diet:	Small mammals, birds, bugs, birds' eggs, and berries
Status:	Threatened

You'd have to head into the shady forest to spot this member of the weasel family. The Newfoundland pine marten prefers to spend its time under a thick canopy of trees rather than open clearings. This helps it stay out of sight, so predators like owls can't spot it from above. An overgrown forest also tends to have fallen trees and a floor littered with leaves, branches, and bark. This makes it a perfect spot for the marten to hide from other predators, like lynx and red foxes, and offers plenty of sites to call home. The Newfoundland marten uses hollow trees, stumps, and rock crevices for its dens and nesting sites.

FACT FILE:

◊ The Newfoundland pine marten is about the size of a small housecat. Unlike other martens, it has a distinctive yellowish-orange patch of fur on its throat and chest.

◊ While it's quick on land, the marten is also an expert at tree climbing. It has sharp claws that help it scurry up trees and run along branches.

◊ Although it climbs trees, the marten hunts mainly on the ground. It searches for its next meal under downed trees and inside hollow logs.

◊ Baby martens, or kits, are born in March and April. There are usually between two and six kits in a litter. Mom cares for her babies alone and rarely leaves the den for the first few months after their birth. The kits set out into the wild with their mom around June, and they'll head off on their own by the time they're about six months old.

HOW'S IT DOING?

The Newfoundland marten was once listed as endangered, but its population has increased and now sits around six hundred. Luckily, large areas of its habitat are now protected, so the mature forests where it lives can thrive, and the marten can safely roam. But the species still faces threats from snaring and trapping outside these areas. It's illegal to trap the marten, but hunters setting out to capture other animals often accidentally trap a marten.

PACIFIC STELLER'S JAY

Habitat: Forests of Haida Gwaii, a group of islands off the coast of British Columbia

Diet: Seeds, nuts, insects, birds' eggs, and berries

Status: Stable

This bird belongs to a family that includes crows, ravens, and blue jays. Unlike its blue jay relative, this jay has made its way to the dark side. At least, when it comes to its colouring. It has a charcoal-black head and neck, and a body that's dark blue. The birds live in flocks that will join together to fend off a predator, like a hawk. They use a method called *mobbing*, which means the birds gather in large numbers and fly at the enemy as they shriek loudly. It's their way of saying "Hey, back off!" And it often works.

FACT FILE:

◊ The Pacific Steller's jay often hops along the forest floor looking for food. Sometimes it heads to the treetops and robs other birds' nests, taking their eggs and making a meal of them.

◊ It makes a variety of calls, but this jay is also good at imitating other animals. For instance, it's known to mimic the call of the red-tailed hawk as well as those of squirrels. Experts believe one of the reasons it does this is to warn other jays that a predator is nearby. While it's usually noisy, the jay does settle down and become very quiet when it's raising its young in a nest.

◊ Male and female Pacific Steller's jays pair up and often stay together for life. The couple teams up to build a nest high in a tree. Using dry leaves, twigs, weeds, and moss, the jays make a cup-shaped nest and glue it together with mud. They line their nest with grasses and pine needles.

◊ A female jay lays between two and five eggs in a nest, and both parents care for the hatchlings. While the young leave the nest about twenty days after hatching, their parents continue to bring them food for another month or so. After that, the little birds are on their own.

HOW'S IT DOING?

The Pacific Steller's jay population is not under any threat. In fact, its population has increased in the past three decades. The bird does a good job of adapting to changes in its habitat, so that keeps its numbers strong.

PEARY CARIBOU

Habitat:	Arctic islands of the Northwest Territories and Nunavut
Diet:	Dried grasses, plants, and low-growing shrubs
Status:	Threatened

Clomping through the Arctic tundra, the Peary caribou roams with a herd of fewer than twenty others of its species. In the cool summer months, it forages for food in river valleys and plains. As winter creeps in, the herd migrates to areas where the snow is not too deep. Since sea ice connects many of the islands in its habitat, the caribou may travel from island to island during the long, harsh winter. They keep a lookout for areas where they may be able to dig up food.

FACT FILE:

◊ Both male and female caribou have antlers covered in fuzzy grey velvet. This velvet is a furry layer of tissue that provides nutrients to the antlers to help them grow quickly. Males shed their antlers in the fall, while females carry theirs through the winter. Antlers are used to attract a mate and help show a caribou's place within a herd. A male's huge antlers tell other herd members that it's strong and in charge.

◊ The Peary caribou uses its hooves to dig through the snow to search for dried grasses to eat. These wide hooves also come in handy in the wintertime. They act like snowshoes, keeping the caribou from sinking in the deep snow.

◊ During the summertime, the Peary caribou enjoys munching on a flowering plant called purple saxifrage. Sometimes its nose is stained red after eating many of the plants.

◊ The caribou is covered in hair. Each hair is hollow (like a straw) and holds warm air close to the skin, which keeps the creature's body warm in the frigid winter.

HOW'S IT DOING?

The Peary caribou lives in a challenging environment, so its population faces struggles. And climate change only adds to the problem. For instance, a series of harsh winters can cause ice layers to build up, making it difficult for a herd to find enough food to survive. Even mild winters can cause difficulties for the caribou. If the sea ice is too thin for the herd to safely walk on, it can't move between islands to forage for food.

COLLARED LEMMING

Habitat: Tundra of central Yukon

Diet: Plants, roots, mosses, berries, and seeds

Status: Imperiled/High Risk of Extinction

During the spring and summer months, the collared lemming's coat is a brownish-grey colour. But come the fall, this small rodent pulls a switch-a-roo. It sheds its fur, and its coat grows back stark white. This white coat helps the lemming camouflage, blending in with its snowy surroundings. That makes it harder for predators like snowy owls and Arctic foxes to track it down. Besides its coat, the rodent also develops a pair of strong front claws as the seasons change. These claws help the lemming dig through snow and ice to reach food buried below. By the time spring arrives, its front claws will have worn down to the same length as its back ones.

FACT FILE:

◊   In winter months, the collared lemming digs into the deep snow to create a seasonal home, known as a burrow. It may hollow out several chambers in its burrow, each with its own purpose. For instance, one may be used as sleeping quarters and another as a bathroom!

◊   Lemmings also build "runways," or pathways, under the snow that allow them to scamper underground as they forage for food.

◊   Like a beaver, a lemming's front teeth never stop growing. But they wear down as they gnaw on hardy plants.

◊   Female lemmings give birth to many little ones through the spring and summer. They can have up to eight young every five weeks, but the average female has about three litters each year. That's a lot of lemmings!

HOW'S IT DOING?

The collared lemming population has its ups and downs. Every three or four years, they suddenly increase in number. So much so that some lemmings migrate to other areas because there isn't enough food to go around. And then, just like that, the number of lemmings plummets—only to slowly increase again. Scientists aren't sure of the reasons for these ups and downs, but these sudden population changes put the lemmings at a higher risk of becoming extinct. Besides being terrible news for lemmings, this could also be a problem for other creatures. Collared lemmings are an important part of the tundra ecosystem. They are a main source of food for many Arctic predators, especially a seabird known as the skua.

HARRIS'S SPARROW

Habitat: Northwest Territories, Nunavut, and northern Manitoba and Saskatchewan

Diet: Berries, seeds, and insects

Status: Special concern

The Harris's sparrow is the lone songbird that breeds only in Canada. It builds its nest on the tundra ground, usually on a small ridge hidden under a shrub or tree. The sparrow scrapes out a small hole and fills it with moss, twigs, and grasses, then lays up to five eggs. These eggs are pale green in colour with reddish-brown spots. The bird's young are ready to leave the nest about ten days after hatching. As September arrives, the Harris's sparrow begins its migration to the central United States. It travels slowly, mostly flying through the night. It takes about two months for the sparrow to arrive in its winter habitat. Since it doesn't breed during its time in the US, it's considered a strictly Canadian bird. The sparrow settles in the south until spring, before it journeys back home to Canada.

FACT FILE:

◊ The Harris's sparrow is the largest sparrow in North America. It measures twenty centimetres long—or about the length of a new pencil.

◊ This sparrow is a brave bird. It forages through patches of vegetation on the ground for its meals, often hopping along in areas where there is no covering from predators. If it senses danger, it quickly flies into a tree or shrub.

◊ When the Harris's sparrow returns to the Canadian tundra in the spring, there are often not many bugs to be found for a meal yet. That's no problem for the Harris's sparrow. It gobbles up crowberries instead. These black-purple berries grow on shrubs in the area. Experts say a female sparrow must eat about 675 berries each day to get the energy she needs. Eat up!

◊ Since this sparrow lives in the remote tundra, it is not often observed in the Canadian wilderness. In fact, the first Harris's sparrow nest was not spotted until 1931, which is much later than most birds living in North America.

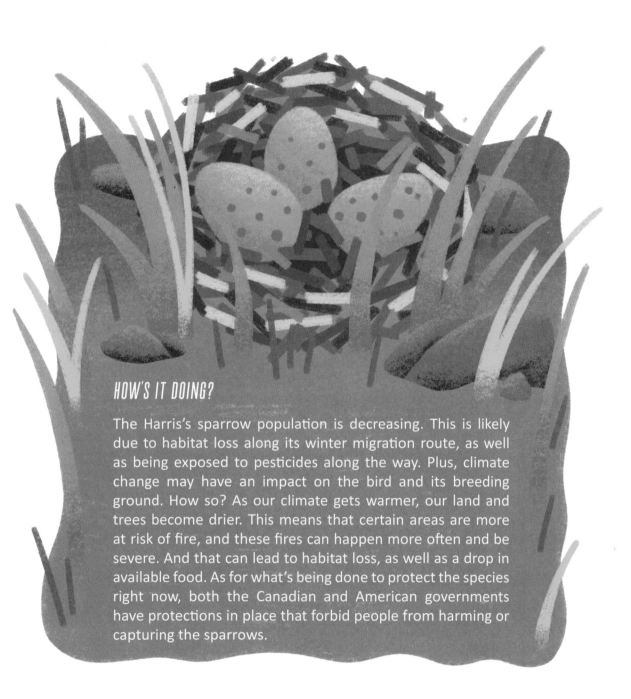

HOW'S IT DOING?

The Harris's sparrow population is decreasing. This is likely due to habitat loss along its winter migration route, as well as being exposed to pesticides along the way. Plus, climate change may have an impact on the bird and its breeding ground. How so? As our climate gets warmer, our land and trees become drier. This means that certain areas are more at risk of fire, and these fires can happen more often and be severe. And that can lead to habitat loss, as well as a drop in available food. As for what's being done to protect the species right now, both the Canadian and American governments have protections in place that forbid people from harming or capturing the sparrows.

WOOD BISON

Habitat: Meadows and forested areas of the Northwest Territories and northern Alberta

Diet: Grasses and ground-growing plants

Status: Special Concern

This huge, hairy beast is the largest land mammal in North America. The wood bison stands up to two metres tall—about the height of an average pro basketball player. And it weighs around the same as a small car! You'd think a creature this big would have a hefty meal plan. But the wood bison is a grazer, which means it feeds on grasses and plants. It eats for several hours each day and then rests a bit. Then it regurgitates—or brings the food back up into its mouth after swallowing it—and chews its meal once more. Sounds gross? Maybe. But eating this way helps the bison digest its food more efficiently.

FACT FILE:

◊ It may seem that a big, lumbering animal like a wood bison wouldn't be able to move quickly. But think again. It's a fast creature, clocking in at speeds of up to fifty-five kilometres an hour. That's about as quick as a zebra!

◊ Wood bison live in herds made up mostly of females and their calves. Male bison graze nearby on their own or in a herd of other males.

◊ During the spring months, the bison sheds its thick winter coat. This leaves it with bare skin and makes it a prime target of flies. To avoid the pesky flies' bites, the bison often looks for a shallow pool of muddy water or a sandy patch on the ground to roll around in and coat its skin. By winter, its coat is back to its full thickness.

◊ Winter weather is no problem for the wood bison. Its thick coat protects it from the cold. And it uses its head to find its dinner. It pushes snow aside with its forehead to find grasses hidden below.

◊ The wood bison may find a home outside of Canada down the road. A herd of 130 wood bison was recently released into the wild in western Alaska. But experts won't know for some time if this new bison population will survive. So for now, Canada is still considered the only home-sweet-home for the wood bison.

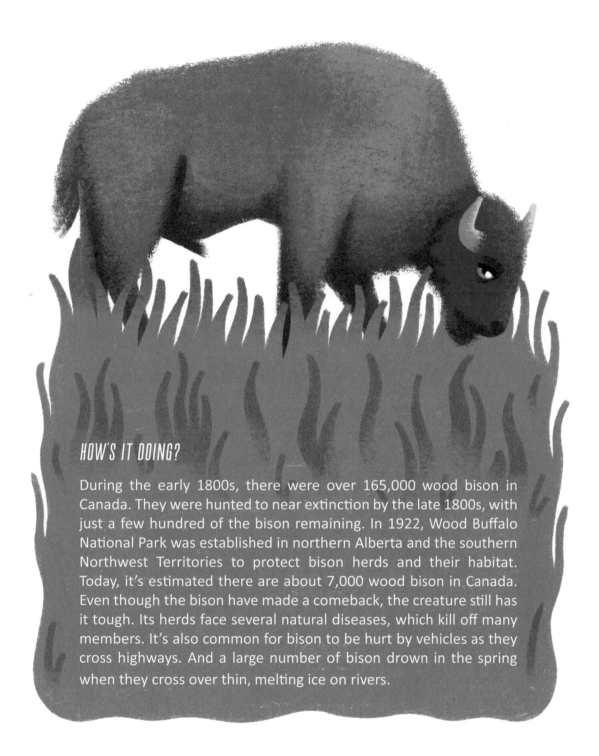

HOW'S IT DOING?

During the early 1800s, there were over 165,000 wood bison in Canada. They were hunted to near extinction by the late 1800s, with just a few hundred of the bison remaining. In 1922, Wood Buffalo National Park was established in northern Alberta and the southern Northwest Territories to protect bison herds and their habitat. Today, it's estimated there are about 7,000 wood bison in Canada. Even though the bison have made a comeback, the creature still has it tough. Its herds face several natural diseases, which kill off many members. It's also common for bison to be hurt by vehicles as they cross highways. And a large number of bison drown in the spring when they cross over thin, melting ice on rivers.

COPPER
REDHORSE

Habitat:	Waterways of southwest Quebec
Diet:	Mollusks like snails and clams
Status:	Endangered

When you hear "copper redhorse," you might picture a brightly coloured horse galloping across a meadow. But redhorses are actually a kind of fish, and you'll find the copper redhorse swimming along the shores of rivers in southwest Quebec. It lives among the grasses that grow in the area's shallow, marshy waters. This is the perfect spot for the copper redhorse to find the food it likes to gobble up—clams and snails. The fish is built to eat creatures like these. It has strong teeth that easily crunch through shells. In fact, these teeth are about the same size as the molars of an adult human!

FACT FILE:

◊ The copper redhorse has large, copper-coloured scales. Its French name is *le chevalier cuivré*, which means "the copper knight," because its scales look like armour.

◊ This fish can grow to be quite big—at least fifty centimetres long, or about the length of a newborn baby. And compared to other Quebec redhorses, it lives the longest. The copper redhorse has a lifespan of about thirty years.

◊ In the spring, when it's ready to spawn, or lay its eggs, the copper redhorse swims upstream to one of two spawning grounds. These areas feature fast-flowing waters. The fish leaves its eggs behind, buried under gravel at the bottom of the river, and swims back to its grassy feeding areas.

◊ So what happens to those eggs? When they hatch, the young remain buried for nearly two weeks until they catch the current to the shallow shores. There, they eat microscopic organisms and grow through the winter before swimming back to the grass beds where adult copper redhorses live.

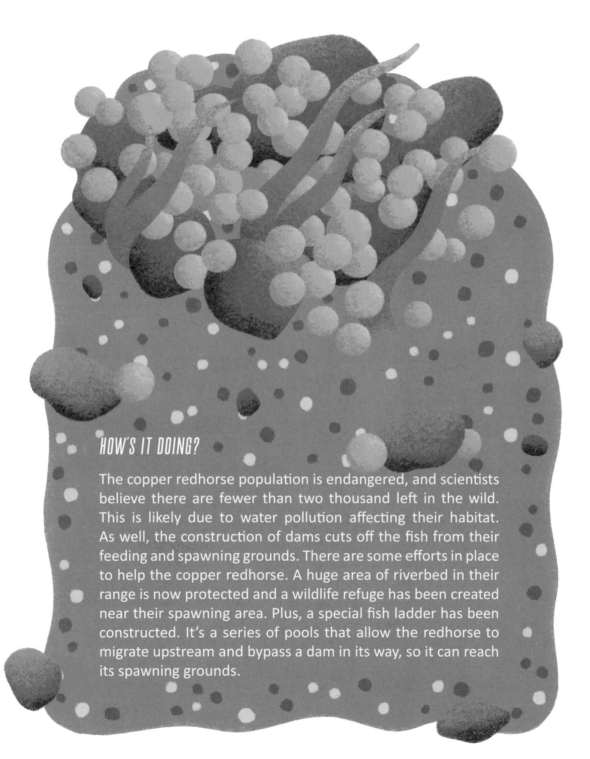

HOW'S IT DOING?

The copper redhorse population is endangered, and scientists believe there are fewer than two thousand left in the wild. This is likely due to water pollution affecting their habitat. As well, the construction of dams cuts off the fish from their feeding and spawning grounds. There are some efforts in place to help the copper redhorse. A huge area of riverbed in their range is now protected and a wildlife refuge has been created near their spawning area. Plus, a special fish ladder has been constructed. It's a series of pools that allow the redhorse to migrate upstream and bypass a dam in its way, so it can reach its spawning grounds.

CONCLUSION

What Can We Do?

Now that we've met some of Canada's endemic species, it's clear many need help. You may be thinking: "I'm a kid. What could I possibly do to save animals that are nowhere near me?" It turns out we can all do something—whether big or small.

Here are a few ideas to get you started:

◊ Create a wildlife habitat in your backyard or schoolyard. Research which plants, trees, and shrubs might help wildlife in your area. Your habitat could also help migrating birds and bugs by providing them with a place to rest and eat. You could even add a birdbath or bat house to your wildlife spot. Make sure you only include things that are healthy and helpful for wildlife—no pesticides or herbicides, please!

◊ Show care and respect for all wildlife and natural habitats. Even those creatures that may creep you out a little—like bees, bugs, or snakes—play an important role in the ecosystem and deserve our respect. If there's a certain creature you're extra creeped out by, try learning more about it—for example, did you know that bats and spiders both eat mosquitos? You might find yourself liking creatures a bit more once you understand how they help.

◊ When you're hiking or spending time at a beach or just at a local park, leave nature how you found it, or a bit better! Litter can be harmful to animals, whether they accidentally eat it or get entangled or injured by it. And garbage can leave behind toxins in our natural world that end up endangering wildlife. You can keep a garbage bag in your backpack just in case you find litter when you're out.

Climate change is a big problem, but all of us can make small changes at home to help. You can try:

◊ Planting trees. They help remove carbon dioxide (CO_2) from the air. It's a greenhouse gas that traps heat in the earth's atmosphere. This causes the earth to warm up and contributes to climate change.

◊ Conserving energy. Turn off lights, TVs, video games, and computers when they're not being used. You can also unplug phone and laptop chargers when they're not in use, so they stop sucking up energy. The great thing about having good energy habits is that you might influence your family and friends too!

◊ Biking or walking when you can, rather than travelling somewhere in a car or bus.

◊ Reducing and reusing as much as you can, and recycling whenever possible.

◊ Sending a letter, postcard, or picture to a government official asking them to focus on climate change and help make a difference.

Keep learning about the creatures around you—both near and far away. You might even volunteer with a wildlife organization or support one that's doing good work. For instance, try joining Parks Canada's Citizen Science projects, save animals with the Earth Rangers conservation program, or get in touch with a local nature centre to see what events they have going on. You never know, there could be a species in your neighbourhood that needs some help.

As you can see, every small act helps. It's all about being a responsible citizen on our one-and-only planet Earth. Together, we can do our part for our world and its creatures!

Grace McDonald

Maria Birmingham has worked in the children's publishing industry for over 25 years. She is the award-winning author of several books for young people, including *Snooze-O-Rama: The Strange Ways that Animals Sleep* and *A Beginner's Guide to Immorality*. She lives in Brampton, Ontario, with her family.

Applehead Studios

Alex MacAskill is a Halifax-based designer and illustrator, often working under the moniker of his studio, Midnight Oil Print & Design House. Alex works on a broad scope of projects from editorial illustration, to developing brand identities, to creating gig posters. His work is inspired by process, textures, the history of illustration and print, and all things organic, which is often why his work is screenprinted or letterpress printed by hand. Alex has always had a strong love for animals and the environment, and you often can find him with a pair of binoculars, birdwatching with his wife and two cats. *midnight-oil.ca*.